LOVE YOURSELF
LOVE IS A FEELING TO BE LEARNED

Love Yourself

Love Is a Feeling to Be Learned

Walter Trobisch

Quiet Waters Publications
Bolivar, Missouri
2001

For information contact
    Quiet Waters Publications,
    Bolivar MO 65613-0034
    E-mail: QWP@usa.net.
For prices and order information visit:
    http://www.quietwaterspub.com

First QWP edition 2001

ISBN 1-931475-06-7
Library of Congress Control Number: 2001119327

LOVE
YOURSELF

loving myself

when i love you more
than i love myself
i am really loving you less

loving myself less than you
i make it harder
for you to love me

your love for me
is so very dependent
on the love i have for myself

and my love for you
will be stronger
if you love yourself the way you love me

—Ulrich Schaffer[1]

DO I LOVE MYSELF?

A young woman entered our hotel room. It was the day after my wife and I had given a lecture at a university in northern Europe. The hotel room was the only place available for counseling.

She was a beautiful Scandinavian woman. Long blond hair fell over her shoulders. Gracefully, she sat down in the armchair offered to her and looked at us with deep and vivid blue eyes. Her long arms allowed her to fold her hands over her knees. We noticed her fine, slender fingers, and we sensed in her a tender, precious personality.

"I Am a Beautiful Woman"

As we discussed her problems, we returned again and again to one issue which seemed to be at the root of all the others. It was a problem we least expected when she entered the room: She could not love herself. In fact, she hated herself to such a degree that she was only one step away from putting an end to her life.

Pointing out her obvious gifts—her success as a student, the favorable impression she had made upon us when first meeting her—seemed to be of no avail. She refused to acknowledge one good thing about herself. She was afraid that any self-appreciation would give in to the temptation of pride, and she believed that God would reject those who are proud. She had grown up in a tight-laced religious family and had learned that self-deprecation was Christian, and self-reproach the only way to find acceptance by God.

We asked her to stand up and take a look at herself in the mirror. She turned her head away. With gentle force I held her head so that she had to look into her own eyes. She cringed as if she were experiencing physical pain.

It took a long time before she was able to whisper, though without conviction, the sentence I asked her to repeat, "I am a beautiful woman."

Loving Ourselves

It is an established fact that we are not born with the ability to love ourselves.

The German psychotherapist Dr. Guido Groeger summarizes the findings of modern psychology by saying,

The opinion seems to be widespread that everyone loves him- or herself, and that all that is necessary is to remind people constantly to love others.

The psychologist has to underline the fact that there is in humans no inborn self-love. Self-love is either acquired or it is nonexistent. The one who does not acquire it or who acquires it insufficiently either cannot love others at all or love them only unsatisfactorily. The same is also true for that person's relationship to God.

It is true that the foundation for this ability to accept oneself is laid in early childhood. But it is also true that an adult needs the assurance of being affirmed and accepted—sometimes to a greater and sometimes to a lesser degree, depending upon the different situations of his or her life.

Because this affirmation is often withheld—especially in Christian circles—a type of Christian is created who loves out of duty and who in this way tortures not only others, but also himself.

Often the choice of a profession is motivated by such a deficiency of love. One hopes to satisfy one's own needs by satisfying the needs of others. But this is a miscalculation.[2]

The Catholic philosopher, Romano Guardini, writes in his essay, "The Acceptance of Oneself," in a similar way.

The act of self-acceptance is the root of all things. I must agree to be the person who I am. Agree to the qualifications which I have. Agree to live within my limits. ... The clarity and the courageousness of this acceptance is the foundation of all existence.[3]

If both these statements are true, that on the one hand self-acceptance is the foundation of all existence, and on the other hand no one is born with the ability to accept and love oneself, we stand before a tremendous challenge, and we have to ask ourselves these questions:

Have I fully and completely accepted myself?

Have I accepted my gifts? My limits? My spiritual, my emotional, my physical dangers?

Have I accepted my lot in life? My gender? My sexuality? My age?

Do I say yes to my marriage? My children? My parents? To being single?

Do I say yes to my economic situation? My state of health? The way I look?

In short, do I love myself?

Psychologists and counselors have commonly begun to replace the word *love* with the word *acceptance*. I regard this as helpful since the word *love* is often abused and thus has become trite and meaningless. The word *acceptance* avoids both the misunderstood romantic and sentimental notion of love as well as viewing it as something merely sexual. To love means, first of all, to accept the other as he or she really is.

And this was precisely one of the problems of our student visitor in that hotel room. She could not get along with anyone, not her fellow students, nor her professors, not even her neighbors, or her own family. She was consumed by hostility and criticism.

When we asked her for an explanation she blamed it all on herself. She said she loved herself too much, thought only of herself and was therefore an egotist. That's why she could not accept and really love others.

We had to contradict her. We claimed just the opposite was true. The reason it was difficult for her to love others was because she did not love herself enough. It is impossible for us to accept the other person as he or she really is if we have not accepted ourselves as we really are.

Love Yourself!

This sheds a new light on the commandment which Jesus emphasized as ranking in importance next to loving God: "Love others as much as you love yourself" (Mt. 22:39; Mk. 12:31; Lk. 10:27).[4]

The Bible first mentions this commandment in Leviticus 19:18. Furthermore, the New Testament mentions it three times. Each time it becomes increasingly clear: Galatians 5:14 calls it a commandment which summarizes the "whole law;" James 2:8 describes it as a fulfillment of the "royal law;" and Romans 13:9 declares it the summation of "all the commandments." When re-reading these passages, note this striking consistency: not once is the commandment *love others* given without the commandment *love yourself*.

This passage is generally interpreted like this: everyone loves him- or herself. Therefore, everyone is an egotist. And since this is wrong, we should love our neighbor instead of ourselves.

Precisely that, however, is *not* stated. It does not read, "Love others *instead* of yourself," but quite the opposite, "Love others *as much as* you love yourself." Self-love is assumed to be an effortless prerequisite and certainly not condemned. Moreover, it is elevated to be the standard for our behavior toward our neighbor, a measure given to us for loving others.[5]

We find that the Bible confirms what modern psychology has recently discovered: without self-love, there can be no love for others. Both are inseparably united in Jesus' commandment of love.

How could Jesus assume that self-love was already naturally present in his listeners? Dr. Groeger, in contrast, states that self-love is not innate, but must be arduously acquired during the course of a lifetime. Part of the answer may lie in the fact that compared to our day, people of Jesus' time were more tranquil and less anxious. They found it easier to acquire self-acceptance, to rest in themselves, and simply to like themselves. Therefore, Jesus could assume that his listeners had learned to accept themselves to an extent that people today have yet to learn. What was presumed as a natural characteristic in their time is more difficult for us to acquire.

Could it be that the difficulty of loving ourselves has become one of the negative by-products of modern civilization?

I have to think of many of my African friends. For them it seems so effortless to accept themselves as they are. One of my best friends, an African man, is rather short. A well-meaning person suggested he wear shoes with higher heels in order to appear taller.

This offended my friend. Hadn't God created him short? Why should he seek to change what God had created? He had accepted himself as he was, and he loved himself including his height. This complete self-acceptance makes him so dear to me.

The love commandment of Jesus, as I see it, contains not only the command *love others* with the assumption *you do also love yourself*, but it contains another command: *love yourself!* Or, to put it into a modern perspective: *accept yourself!* Only those who accept themselves can accept others. Only those who love themselves can love others.

I would like to mention two Bible passages in this context. In the description of the friendship between David and Jonathan, we find this thought-provoking sentence, "Jonathan thought as much of David as he did of himself" (1 Sam 18:1). This means: Jonathan loved himself and that enabled his deep friendship with David.

I ask myself: Do I have the courage to love my own soul? Do I sometimes talk to my soul as David did in Psalm 103? "Bless the Lord, O my soul: and all that is within me, bless his holy name. Bless the

Lord, O my soul, and forget not all his benefits"
(KJV). Or do I lack that courage out of fear?

And what does this all have to do with marriage?
Everything. In Ephesians 5:21-33, Paul's famous
passage about marriage, self-love is mentioned no
less than three times. In verse 28 we read, "In the
same way, a husband should love his wife as much as
he loves himself. A husband who love his wife
shows that he loves himself." And verse 29 says,
"None of us hate our own bodies. We provide for
them and take good care of them …" Finally, verse
33 states, "So each husband should love his wife as
much as he loves himself …"

I must admit that I had preached many times about
this text before this simple statement really struck
me: Whoever loves his wife, loves himself. This certainly cannot mean that whoever loves his wife is
egocentric. On the contrary, whoever loves his wife
proves that he has acquired self-acceptance and thus
has learned to love himself. And the same can be
said for any woman who loves her husband. And it
is interesting that Paul explicitly mentions the physical dimension of self-acceptance.

I ask myself: Do I love my own body? Or do I lack
the courage because of fear or even misguided
spirituality? Do I really love myself, body and soul?

Self-Love and Selflessness

I can well imagine that many readers who have followed my thoughts thus far may have become a bit nervous and uncomfortable. Does my advice not contradict what we have been brought up to believe as good Christians? Is it not written, "If you love your life, you will lose it" (John 12:25)? "You cannot come with me unless you love me more than you love your own life" (Luke 14:26). "If any of you want to be my followers, you must forget about yourself ..." (Mt. 16:24).

Indeed, as Christians we have been conditioned with concepts of self-denial and self-sacrifice, and with fear of being egotistical. The idea that the plea to love oneself seems almost a blasphemy is ingrained into us. What then is the distinction between self-love and selfishness, between self-acceptance and egotism?

One difficulty lies in the double meaning of the word self-love, that of self-acceptance and of self-centeredness. Accordingly, Josef Pieper stresses in his essay *Zucht und Maß*: "There are two opposing ways in which humans can love themselves: selflessly or selfishly. Only the first is self-preserving, while the second is self-destroying."

An example of self-love in the negative sense is illustrated by the Greek myth about Narcissus. He was a youth who, while gazing at his reflection in a well, fell in love with himself. Totally absorbed with his own image, he tumbled into the water and drowned. From this myth, the word narcissism is derived. Another Greek term for *self* and *love* which conveys the same idea is autoeroticism.

Self-love in the positive sense of self-acceptance is the exact opposite of narcissism or autoeroticism. It actually resembles a prerequisite for a first step toward true selflessness. We cannot give to others what we do not have ourselves. Only when I have accepted my *self* can I let go of it, can I become selfless. If, however, I have not found my *self* and not discovered my own identity, then I must keep on searching. I become literally self-centered, egocentric.

Let me put it bluntly: *if I do not love myself, I am an egotist.* I must become an egotist necessarily because I am not sure of my identity, and I am therefore always trying to find myself. Like Narcissus, who was engrossed with himself, I become completely self-centered.

The Nobel Prize winning novel of Hermann Hesse, *Steppenwolf,* describes the intricate relationship between a lack of self-love (which he calls self-hate) and an escalation in self-centeredness (which he calls "sheer egoism") or, rather, the inability to love others. He says about Harry Hailer, the hero of the novel:

As for others and the world around him he never ceased in his heroic and earnest endeavor to love them, to be just to them, to do them no harm, for the love of his neighbor was as strongly forced upon him as the hatred of himself, and so his whole life was an example that the love of one's neighbor is not possible without love of oneself, and that self-hate is really the same thing as sheer egoism, and in the long run breeds the same cruel isolation and despair.[6]

This sheds light on modern man's search for identity. In his search, Harry Hailer employs various means such as drinking, overeating, tripping, and experimenting with sex. All these express the lack of self-acceptance. Those infatuated with themselves believe that they will find their identity within the magical time-span of dream and drunkenness, within self-gratification through alcohol, excess of food, drugs, or sex; but that will leave them even less satisfied and set off yet another compulsion in their addictive self-search. Our time and age is marked by so much addiction and infatuation with our own self because truthful self-love, self-finding, and self-acceptance is relentlessly suppressed.

Self-love excludes self-infatuation. Love "seeketh not her own" (I Cor. 13:5 KJV) for love has found her own. I can give only what I have, let go of only what I hold, lose only what I possess, deny only what I am, and hate only what I love. The Bible refers to the word *hate* not as emotional hatred, but as the ability to distance oneself from wishes and desires without self-regard. To *hate* in Aramaic means: to *put in second place*. Self-love is necessary before we can be freed from ourselves.[7]

Self-love means *I love myself*, I am able to look beyond myself. Autoeroticism means *I love I*, I am incapable of looking beyond my own self, and I continually return back to it. Self-love must be attained, whereas autoeroticism is innate.

All of us experience the autoerotic phase before we are five years old and again at the onset of puberty. If we remain in this self-centered phase, however, we will not acquire true self-love.

Being infatuated with, or having a crush on someone, is an emotional manifestation of the autoerotic phase. The adolescent often has an idol with whom he or she is in love and onto whom one's own identity is projected. Adolescents love the image of themselves which they see in the other person, just as Narcissus loved his reflection in the well. The dream is shattered the moment the idol is viewed from a realistic stance and becomes incompatible with the adolescent's projected image.

Jesus and Self-Acceptance

The relationship between self-love and selflessness, between self-acceptance and self-denial, is best illustrated by the example we have in Jesus Christ. Jesus wholly knew himself, and he was completely in harmony with himself. With absolute authority he could say, "Even before Abraham was, I was, and I am" (John 8:58). And along with the God who called himself, "I Am" (Exodus 3:14), Jesus declared, "I am one with the Father." (John 10:30)

It is interesting to note that, in the New Testament, statements regarding Christ's identity precede statements concerning his self-denial. For example, before Jesus washed his disciples' feet, there is a splendid declaration of his total self-acceptance: "Jesus knew that he had come from God and would go back to God. He also knew that the Father had given him complete power" (John 13:3).

Self-acceptance and selflessness are completely in-
terconnected. Jesus knew who he was, and he accepted his identity and purpose. Self-acceptance was
an intrinsic part of his life, enabling him to turn his
attention outwards and to love truly the people with
whom he came into contact. It was unnecessary for
him to keep stressing his identity, his equality with
God, like something he had taken that did not really
belong to him. Rather, "he gave up everything and
became a slave, when he became one of us. Christ
was humble. He obeyed God and even died on a
cross" (Phil. 2:7-8).

Here too Jesus' self-denial is preceded by a statement of his identity, "Christ was truly God" (Phil.
2:6). Through this complete interconnection the Bible asserts: There is no neighborly love without self-
love. In other words, since Jesus loved himself, he
was both selfless and able to love others "as he loved
himself."

That's easy enough for Jesus, we might say, but for
us? Paul's appeal to this hesitation of ours is con-
vincing: "think the same way that Christ Jesus
thought" (Phil. 2:5).

If Jesus Christ is our life, then the acceptance of
ourselves is indeed "the foundation of all existence,"
as Guardini would say. Discipleship is not possible

without it. The obedience of self-denial presupposes
the obedience of self-acceptance.

Learning to Love Ourselves

If it is true that self-love is the foundation of our
love for others, and if it is true that it is not innate
but must be acquired, then we face a difficult question, "How can I learn to accept myself, to love myself?"

To this question there is only one answer, one that
is really quite simple: by learning to let myself be
loved. I can only accept myself once I am accepted; I
can only love myself once I am loved and let myself
be loved. Martin Buber says, "Only through others
will we find ourselves."

The other day I observed a woman who received a
compliment about a nice dress she was wearing. She
shrugged off the compliment by saying, "Oh, this is
just an old thing I've had hanging in my closet for
years." Even if this was true—and very likely it was
not—it was clear to me that she had not learned to
welcome appreciation, to *accept* acceptance.

The counterexample is that of a woman we know
who keeps a journal of all of her enjoyable experiences. She also records compliments she has re-

ceived from members of her family or friends. One day her four-year-old told her, "You are the best Mommy in the world." Whenever she feels down or depressed, she opens this journal to bring joy to herself.

It seems to me that we are inclined to ward off any expressions of praise because of a misconception of Christian modesty and humility. We even tend to distrust those who praise us, and we doubt the motives behind their affirmation. And thus we discourage those who love us until they give up expressing their love. As a consequence we deprive ourselves of the experience of being loved, an experience so necessary for learning to love ourselves.

Michelangelo wrote to the woman he loved: "When I am yours, then I am at last wholly myself." This lays emphasis on Paul's statement on marriage in Ephesians 5:28: "A husband should love his wife as much as he loves himself." Let me paraphrase it: "He who is loved by his wife learns to love himself."

Fortunate are those who have learned this complete acceptance as babies at their mothers' breasts. Not only physically but also emotionally their needs have been met. They feel safe and develop basic trust on which self-love and self-acceptance is founded.

We need love and acceptance throughout our lives, not only in infancy and childhood, but as adults too. We all know how heartened we are by a word of recognition or affirmation in our daily work. No one is able to work well without these acknowledgements of our efforts every now and then. It is as necessary and sustaining as bread is for our daily life.

All of us need the "daily bread" of praise, and it is precisely this "daily bread" which we tend to withhold from each other. We are quick to criticize and slow to praise. Often we express only negative remarks, and in this way, we destroy the self-confidence of those around us.

In an atmosphere where praise is withheld, we often encounter persons who, as Dr. Groeger put it, "love out of duty," who cannot love themselves because they experienced little love and little praise. Their love does not spring from joy but is forced or, as Hermann Hesse puts it, is the result of a "heroic and earnest endeavor."

Have we not been in this same position ourselves from time to time? We don't feel like loving someone, yet we charge ourselves, "I should love, I should love, I should love!" It is like doing spiritual chin-ups in an effort to please others and to please God. However, we all know how it is with chin-ups.

For a limited time, we can pull ourselves up, but then, inevitably, the moment comes when we run out of strength and have to stop. A car that runs out of gas may be pushed a short distance, but not very far, especially not uphill.

When I was in Africa, one of my fellow missionaries constructed a windmill. He planned to draw water out of a deep well by means of wind power. The idea was great. When there was no wind, however, we had no water. A man on a bicycle had to produce the power. It is easy to imagine how quickly he became exhausted.

Persons who love out of duty are like the man on the bicycle. They try to produce love by their own effort. They receive no strength from outside. They cannot love others because they are neither loved nor praised by others. And since they do not love, they will not be loved and praised either.

A Vicious Circle

This leads us to an even more daunting question: if it is true that we can only learn self-acceptance by letting ourselves be accepted, then we are exposed to a vicious circle.

We can only accept each other once we have accepted ourselves. Yet, we can only accept ourselves
once we are accepted. We can only love ourselves
once we are loved.

And so, the circle starts all over.

What happens if we have never been loved? If the
deficiency of love has never been replenished? What
happens to children who grow up without the
warmth and security of a loving home, without parents who care for, love, and spend time with them?
And what happens if in school and at their job they
get only reproof and criticism? If it is true that we
can only find our own self through others, what
happens if *others* are simply not present?

Are such persons destined to a life of hopeless solitude, to a flight into addictions and self-gratifications
of any kind? The vicious circle then starts to spin:
they cannot love—either themselves or others—
because they are not loved, and they are not loved
because they fail to love.

Breaking Through the Vicious Circle

Psychology and philosophy competently describe
and explain this vicious circle, but these sciences
cannot break through from within to help us get out.

The circle must be broken through and shattered from the outside.

In Romans 15:7, the Apostle Paul identifies the source capable of breaking through from the outside: "Honor God by accepting each other, as Christ has accepted you."

Jesus Christ is the one who breaks through the vicious circle. He has broken it from the outside. Now we have a base on which we can firmly stand. Jesus Christ accepts us as we are, fully, wholly, and unconditionally. He thus makes it possible for us to accept ourselves and to accept one another.

There are certainly many weighty and justified questions concerning the practice of infant baptism. Yet, it conveys one message clearly: God has accepted me unconditionally, even before I could do a thing. In the throes of deep doubts, Martin Luther—himself deprived of warmth and love as a child and struggling with self-acceptance throughout his whole life—took a piece of chalk and wrote in large print on his desk, "I have been baptized."

Through Christ, God has taken the initiative in love. He spoke the first word. He took the first step. Therefore, we can love ourselves and others as He has loved us: "We love, because he first loved us" (1 John 4:19).

The question is this: "How much does this fact mean to me, personally? Does it mean enough to me so that I can stop blaming my childhood experiences, or my past, or my treatment by other people for my inability to love? Has God's love become so real that it even replaces love withdrawn from me?"

Those who allow themselves to be found by Christ will find themselves. They can accept themselves as they are, all-inclusive; not only their favorable, beneficial characteristics, but also the negative, disadvantageous ones.

The parents of a distinguished family phoned us. Their son was hospitalized after an unsuccessful suicide attempt.

"I am going to do it again" was the first thing he told us when my wife and I visited him.

"Why?"

"I am an error, a mistake. I am not supposed to exist." We did not understand.

Slowly, the full story emerged. He had overheard a hideous argument of his parents in which he learned that he was an unwanted child. His mother had forgotten to take the pill, and in anger his father reminded her of it and blamed her for it.

This experience had crushed him. What was the meaning, the purpose, of his life, if he was not supposed to be alive in the first place? If his parents did not want him, who else did?

What about God? Does God want all children to be born who are born? Even if their parents did not want them to be born? These questions had been weighing too heavily on him and led him to attempt suicide.

"God wants you," we assured him.

"How do you know?" He looked at us. His eyes expressed both doubt and hope at the same time.

"God was himself an unwanted child," I answered, "unexpected and unplanned, an embarrassment to his parents. He came to this world without their actions—let alone their desire. Furthermore, he remained an unwanted person throughout his life—until they tried to take him out of this world by crucifying him."

"And still," my wife added, "there has never been a child more desired, more loved by God, and never a person who became a greater blessing to more people than Jesus."

The face of the young man expressed unbelieving amazement. "Me, a blessing?"

"Yes, a special blessing," we assured him.

Never had we understood more profoundly the intervention of God into the vicious circle. God, himself completely cast out, looks after the outcasts. God, himself undesired, wants the undesired. God, himself unloved, loves the unloved. God, who himself has become human, wants to live within every human being. Acceptance, therefore, exists for everyone.

We prayed together with the young man and witnessed his acceptance of God's acceptance.

Love Is More than Acceptance

So far, I have used the words *love* and *acceptance* interchangeably. Love, however, is more than mere acceptance.

Christ accepts us as we are: "Everything and everyone that the Father has given me will come to me, and I won't turn any of them away" (John 6:37). But when he accepts us, we cannot remain as we are. Acceptance is nothing but the first step of love. Then it exposes us to a process of growth. Being accepted by the love of Christ means being transformed.

In this aspect the verse of John 1:12 has been newly revealed to me, and I would like to paraphrase it like this: "Those who welcome Christ, who slowly learn to surrender their lives to him, who let themselves be loved will receive strength to work on themselves becoming children of God and growing into the image God has intended for them."

In his fourth thesis, which he nailed on the church door in Wittenberg, Luther stated, "God's love does not love that which is worthy of love, but it creates that which is worthy of love." Love works and shapes; it carves out the image which God has intended—and that is a lifelong process. To be accepted by God does not mean: "You are just the way you are, and nothing can be done about that." Instead, it means: "I accept you as you are, but now the work of love begins. I need your cooperation—your self-love."

Someone asked me in confusion, "Isn't this a contradiction? On one hand I should accept myself as I am—agree to be the person I am. On the other hand I should work on myself, I should change and grow?"

My answer is this: God's love does not free us from working on ourselves, it enables us to do that work. To let God accept me does not imply sitting back passively with the attitude, "This is just the way I am—I can't do anything about it." Instead, it means that I expose myself to a difficult process of growth, and that I let God's chisel of love to work on me. Self-acceptance, therefore, is only the first step, the starting point—although one of profound and indispensable significance. Self-acceptance does not relieve me from working on myself, but on the contrary, it compels and enables me to do that work.

Dr. Theodor Bovet writes, "If I truly love myself, I am unable to stand still. I will want to change to become the one whom God desires me to become. In the same way we should also love our neighbor."[8]

Critics of my book *I Loved a Girl*,[9] have accused me of not accepting François—the young man with whom I was corresponding—and of trying to change him. Actually, I did accept him, as the first letters show. Then, however, I challenged him to change his ways precisely because I loved him. Love has a dimension beyond mere acceptance. When I love my neighbor 'as much as I love myself,' then I want to see my neighbor become all that God created him or her to be.

THE CONSEQUENCES OF
INADEQUATE SELF-LOVE

If we love ourselves in the wrong way, then it is impossible to grow and develop into the people God wants us to be. Many problems in our lives and in our dealings with others result from the lack of self-love. I have already discussed the search for self-identity through drinking, eating, drugs, and experimenting with sex. But other problems can also result from inadequate self-love.

The Autoerotic Choice of Profession and Partner

The choice of entering social-work professions may be motivated by the desire to be needed. It often stems from an unconscious attempt to make up for a deficiency of love. By placing ourselves in a position where we are needed by others, unloved people attempt to fulfill their own needs and bolster their own self-concept.

This, however, is a miscalculation. Such helpers cannot really help, for they desire the ones in need more than the needy ones need them. These helpers just become more entangled with themselves and have no ability to understand the ones in need.

Similarly, the choice of a life partner can be an attempt to make up for a deficiency of love. Such a choice will always result in a very difficult marriage. An individual who cannot love him or herself will challenge his or her spouse with insatiable demands and long for the love of the other one without being either able or willing to give something in return. Cruel as it may sound, marriage is no hospital for love-cripples. A deficiency of self-love is not cured just by getting married.

Hostility toward the Body

If I am unable to accept myself, I am also unable to accept my body. Hostility toward the body is always a symptom of the lack of self-love. Those who do not love themselves, do not love their body either.

In his book *A Place for You*, Dr. Paul Tournier gives two examples of such a negative attitude toward the body:

A pretty woman confides in me that her first act when entering a hotel room is to turn all mirrors with their faces to the wall. Another tells me that she has never been able to look at herself naked without a feeling of shame. "This body of mine," she adds, "is my enemy." [10]

These women were unable to accept their own bodies because they were unable to accept themselves.

Such hatred for one's body will naturally have a negative effect on marriage. As I have already mentioned, in Ephesians 5 the Apostle Paul emphasizes specifically the physical dimension of self-acceptance. Marriage problems in the sexual realm are often associated with the fact that at least one of the partners has difficulty in accepting his or her body as it is.

Could that be the reason why so many Christians fail to achieve sexual harmony in marriage? Many Christians seem to have the attitude that their physical relationship is somewhat worldly, even sinful, and somehow less recognized in God's eyes than their spiritual fellowship. They believe that the body is less pleasing to God than the soul. It is not surprising that such an unhealthy attitude toward the body affects their physical harmony.

Church or social circles, which stress man's sinfulness, often regard healthy self-love as sinful pride. A deeply seated contempt or even hatred of the body is the result. Adherents to that theology will hardly go to a gym, let alone take dance lessons, although doing so could help significantly in developing a positive self-image of the body and overcoming this particular neurosis.

As Dr. Tournier writes,

Gymnastics, especially the dance, singing, and all the arts of bodily self-expression, have great therapeutic value. It is not a matter of accepting willy-nilly that one has a body, but of rediscovering its value, of using it as a genuine manifestation of one's person, and of becoming aware once more of its spiritual significance. The body is the place of love. The sex act is not merely the expression of one's feelings, but the sublime gift of oneself, a true spiritual testament.[11]

An additional aid for women, single or married, who wish to learn to love themselves and their bodies is to live consciously in harmony with her menstrual cycle. The cycle is as unique and individual as one's fingerprint. This is why the intimate knowledge of its unique characteristics can help women considerably in finding their identity.[12]

Hostility toward Children

When traveling from country to country, w struck by the increasing hostility toward children throughout the world. Interestingly, this is less prevalent in countries of the Third World than it is in the so-called "Christian West."

I remember when we came home from Africa to Germany with five children of kindergarten and grade-school age. It was next to impossible for us to find a place to live, for the children a place to play, and for all of us a place where we could spend our vacations together. In Finland, we met young couples with two children who would have wanted a third child (and there is certainly no overpopulation in Finland!), but they were afraid of being ostracized by society. In America too we have met mothers who were ashamed because they had become pregnant a third time.

It seems to me that there is a direct relationship between the lack of self-acceptance, the hostility toward the body, and the hostility toward children. Bringing forth children is a part of the physical dimension of life. Those without a positive relationship with their body will find it difficult to attain a positive relationship with the child—a fruit of their body.

My wife Ingrid and I, after talks with troubled women (and men) throughout the world, wonder whether one of the deepest roots of the abortion problem does not lie here. Could it be that this also is the result of lacking self-acceptance which expresses itself in a hostile act against the unborn fruit of the body?

Over-Eating and Under-Eating

It is peculiar, but it seems to me that, while men require relatively more personal recognition, women find it relatively more difficult to develop a positive relationship toward their bodies. In our many interviews with women who reflect a poor self-image, my wife and I have often discovered two repeatedly occurring symptoms: Either these women eat too much or they eat too little. Both overeating and under-eating are expressions of the same ailment—lack of self-love.

Through the lack of self-love a void is created. Over-eating—or getting drunk—is an attempt to fill this void. For when I am not 'agreeable' to myself, I must make up for this deficiency with other, more 'agreeable' items.

Under-eating, on the other hand, denies the body the nourishment it needs. It may indicate a refusal of *me* to *myself* and thus a wish to get rid of *myself*. However, true freedom from oneself, true "selflessness," cannot be achieved so easily. It can only be accomplished through the longer and more difficult path toward realizing self-love. The wish to be free of oneself is directly linked to suicide, the ultimate expression of hostility toward the body and of the rejection of *one's self*.

Fear

Whoever takes this final drastic step of attempting suicide, demonstrates a greater fear of living than of dying. Fear is also a consequence of a lack of self-love.

"Love seeketh not her own," Paul writes in 1 Corinthians 13:5 (KJV). But those who do not know what love is and cannot love themselves must always 'seek' themselves, constantly pursued by the fear that perhaps they will never discover that for which they are searching. Consequently, the self-centered person tends to be fearful and apprehensive. Such individuals revolve around their own axis, losing sight of all else but themselves and their own interests. In such persons, fear takes root. Egotists feels unsheltered, insecure, unprotected, and at the mercy of a cruel, unloving world. They defensively cling to themselves, afraid that doing otherwise would ensure personal defeat and destruction.

Since fear and self-centeredness are so closely linked, we are susceptible to a currently widespread fear, namely the fear of failure. It is a natural by-product of modern man's idolatry of accomplishment. From early childhood we are indoctrinated with the viewpoint that performance determines worth. When a machine ceases to be productive, it is discarded. Likewise, if we fail to perform at the level expected of us, we are considered useless. There is no tolerance for failures, and so non-achievers become ostracized.

Outcasts, however, cannot love themselves. Those whom society ostracizes cannot acquire self-respect. Those completely deprived of value lose their feeling of self-worth. Yet, self-worth is essential for everyone to live. The fear of failure can therefore become greater than the fear of death.

Once more, we encounter the connection between lack self-love and of suicide. Potentially suicidal individuals feel trapped between their fear of failure and their own self-centeredness. They conclude that the only way to get rid of their fear is to get rid of themselves.

The answer, however, lies not in suicide. It lies in learning how to live with fear.

In this respect I have found a declaration of Jesus most helpful: "In the world you shall have tribulation: but be of good cheer; I have overcome the world" (John 16:33 KJV). The Greek word for tribulation expresses the idea of being pressured, of being trapped. The German translation uses the word *Angst*, which contains the same root found in the words anxiety and anguish. It comes from *Enge* and means strait, narrowness, being in a tight spot, in a bottleneck. All these expressions convey the experience of fear.

The first aid in learning how to handle fear is to stop fighting it. The verse eradicates the myth that, being a Christian, I have to be fearless. Jesus states it clearly and simply: "In the world you shall have tribulation." And that is a matter of fact. Since Jesus speaks this word to his disciples, we are assured that as children of God we may still have fear. But we are liberated from being pressured by fear. We need not *fear* fear. Furthermore, this declaration of Jesus is not followed by some criticism or objection, but instead affirmed by a word of comfort: "Be of good cheer."

I would like to formulate the message using this paradox, "We may be cheerfully fearful."

My own experience during the Second World War taught me how to live with fear. I had to live for days and sometimes even weeks in fear of being killed at any moment. Every single time I heard the roar of the Russian artillery, I knew that the next few seconds would determine whether I would live or die. It was an unrelenting exercise of living with fear.

I remember that the first relief came when I stopped fighting my fear and learned to admit to myself, "Walter, you are afraid." In that moment, the tight grip of fear loosened, and fear became bearable. I experienced it even as a positive force, one that challenged my faith in God.

Faith did not free me from fear, but fear forced me to believe. Each time I heard the roar of the enemy fire, I threw myself down into a trench or a foxhole. I surrendered to the one who has overcome the world, and I said, "I am completely yours." There I learned not to *fear* fear.

It is important to note that Jesus did not say, "I have overcome tribulation. I have overcome fear." Instead, he said, "I have overcome the world." This gives us another decisive aid in dealing with fear, confronting it not directly, but indirectly, similar to the Knight's move in the game of chess. The Knight does not attack his opponent linearly and head-on; instead he has the power to make an L-shaped move, jumping over squares that may be occupied. Similarly, we cannot deal with fear by a head-on attack. We need to surrender to the One who has overcome the world—including our own merciless, achievement-oriented society.

Herein lies our hope and consolation: The One who overcame the world felt fear himself. He lived through such agonies that "his sweat fell to the ground like drops of blood" (Lk. 22:44). The experience of His own fears empowers Christ to rescue us from the domain of fear. He understands our fears, and He loves and accepts us including our fears. He even admonishes us to "cheer up" in the midst of fear and tribulation.

The final chapter, accordingly, is dedicated to depression as a common manifestation of the lack of cheerfulness and self-love.

DEPRESSION AND HELPS IN
OVERCOMING IT

Depression is also a consequence of inadequate self-love, perhaps even the most common one today. The number of depressed people is astonishing. Even more astonishing is the number of depressed Christians. I am not speaking of superficial people, but of many sincere believers who live in a personal relationship with Jesus Christ, and who still struggle continuously with deep depression.

Depression is always connected to a feeling of loss. Outward circumstances may be the cause: the loss of material goods, the loss of health, the loss of a loved one, the loss of confidence, the loss of self-respect because we feel guilty over something, or the loss of a skill perhaps as a result of aging. We react to these experiences with sadness, self-pity, mourning, disap-pointment, envy, shame, and self-depreciation. All these feelings flow together like little brooks into a stream of a general feeling of depression.

Three kinds of depression seem to be increasing. First, a depression which stems from exhaustion. Executives, top-achievers, and over-conscientious housewives suffer in particular from this form of depression. When they cannot achieve perfection, they experience a loss of competence as they realize they cannot accomplish everything alone.

Another form of depression is brought about by moving to a different residence. Even rearranging furniture and redecorating can result in a feeling of loss. One feels uprooted and is acutely aware that one's old home, the four walls one knew so well, is missing.

There is even a depression which stems from the loss of a task, or of a certain burden we had been carrying. Depression resulting from retirement is one variation of this. Strangely enough, it doesn't strike as long as we are burdened by a certain task, but it appears when we least expect it, the moment the burden is finally lifted. When the job has been completed, when the battle has been won, when the exam has been passed, when the tension has been relieved, and the conflict has been solved—then this depression hits us unexpectedly. The loss of a challenge, of our work, or of a struggle plummets us into an aching void.

There is also a depression without apparent, outward causes, one that assails a person from within. It can manifest itself in either restless, nervous energy, or passive inertia which make any constructive action impossible. Such a "depression from inside" is usually accompanied by tormenting self-accusations and exaggerated feelings of guilt. Although no tangible source can be established, ideas of being deprived, underprivileged, unimportant, and inferior persist, and often lead to a complete loss of any feeling of self-worth.

This explains why depressed individuals are so vulnerable and oversensitive when they are confronted with criticism. They cling to other people, and they always long desperately for recognition and the assurance of being loved, to enable them to love themselves.

The deepest root of depression is the feeling that I have lost myself and have given up hope of ever finding myself again. There is nothing in me worth loving. I reach into a void when I try to love myself.

This means that self-acceptance and depression are closely interrelated. The various forms of depression clearly depict a self-centeredness which we recognize as the natural consequence of a lack of self-love.

The best protection against sinking into depression, therefore, is learning to love ourselves. At the same time, overcoming depression is the best approach for attaining self-love.

Depression in the Bible

In overcoming depression, it is encouraging to know that the Bible's understanding of us humans is truly profound.

King Saul was often plagued by depression. He depended upon David, the shepherd boy, to help soothe the depression by playing on the lyre: "The Spirit of the Lord had left Saul, and an evil spirit from the Lord was terrifying him. … Whenever the evil spirit from God bothered Saul, David would play his harp. Saul would relax and feel better, and the evil spirit would go away" (1 Sam. 16:14, 23).

This story contains a helpful suggestion on how to counteract depression. Music conveys harmony and order and thus can heal a mind lost in disorder and disharmony.

Nebuchadnezzar disregarded a dream sent by God. The dream warned him against illusions of grandeur and admonished him to repent. Nebuchadnezzar dismissed the dream and fell into a depression that caused him to live like a wild animal: "I was forced to live like a wild animal; I ate grass and was unprotected from the dew. As time went by, my hair grew longer than eagle feathers, and my fingernails looked like the claws of a bird" (Daniel 4:33).

Nebuchadnezzar, however, relates how he overcame this depression and gives us another helpful suggestion. He tells us of how the act of praise and thanksgiving can heal us: "Finally, I prayed to God in heaven, and my mind was healed. Then I said: 'I praise and honor God Most High. He lives forever, and his kingdom will never end'" (Daniel 4:34).

Elijah, in the account in I Kings 19, is struck by a depression after a spiritually climactic experience, after a great battle for the Lord had been won. In a state of great physical exhaustion, he "came to a large bush and sat down in its shade. He begged the Lord, 'I've had enough. Just let me die! I'm no better off than my ancestors'" (I Kings 19:4).

We can learn a lot from how the Lord dealt with Elijah's depression: no reprimand, no appeal to the will, but instead loving care, rest, food—and physical contact: "Then he lay down in the shade and fell asleep. Suddenly an angel woke him up and said,

'Get up and eat.' Elijah looked around, and by his head was a jar of water and some baked bread. He sat up, ate and drank, then lay down and went back to sleep" (v. 5).

The Apostle Paul was certainly a person prone to depression. Romano Guardini, in his book *The Image of Jesus in the New Testament*, vividly portrays this side of the apostle. This description made Paul much more human to me. Guardini writes about Paul, "He seemed to be a man who attracted that which was difficult, against whom fate seemed to be pitted, a harassed man. ... He had to suffer much, continuously and in all situations."

Paul was a rabbinical student, a discipline which served to nurture his perfectionist tendencies. The same depression—which assaults all top-achievers when they are faced with the reality of their own human limitations and failings—is contained in the undertones of the following sentences: "In fact, I don't understand why I act the way I do. I don't do what I know is right. I do the things I hate. ... I know that my selfish desires won't let me do anything that is good. Even when I want to do right, I cannot. Instead of doing what I know is right, I do wrong" (Romans 7:15, 18-19).

One cannot help but ask the question: "What evil might this man have done to cause him to speak like this?" Walter Uhsadel, professor of theology at Tübingen University, comments on this: "The inner vulnerability of depressed persons causes them to be more aware of their failings and to suffer more under the burden of this knowledge than other people."[13]

Focusing on the last few chapters of II Corinthians, Uhsadel points out another typical symptom of a depressed person, displayed by Paul as he vacillates between boasting and self-devaluation. At the same time, Paul longs deeply for recognition, appreciation, and love, as expressed in II Corinthians 12:11: "I have been making a fool of myself. But you forced me to do it, when you should have been speaking up for me. I may be nothing at all, but I am as good as those super apostles."

The Psalms are where I always feel that the Bible understands us best. The one who prayed Psalm 31, for instance, certainly was well acquainted with depression:

Have pity, Lord! I am hurting and almost blind. My whole body aches. I have known only sorrow all my life long, and I suffer year after year. I am weak from sin, and my bones are limp. (vv. 9-10)

The feeling expressed in this psalm: I am spent, consumed, aching. I am becoming less and less. I am wasting away. Nothing inspires hope. Everything appears desolate and cold. Time crawls slowly along without an end or purpose. We can easily visualize this vast number of sighing Christians suffering like that.

What has been discovered by psychosomatic medicine only recently, the psalmist has experienced long ago. Body and soul are a unity. Grief of the soul means grief of the body. The psalmist's depression literally assails his bones.

My enemies insult me. Neighbors are even worse, and I disgust my friends. People meet me on the street, and they turn and run. I hear the crowds whisper, "Everyone is afraid!" They are plotting and scheming to murder me. (vv. 11, 13)

This feeling: I am threatened, trapped. I have only enemies. Everyone is against me; nobody understands me. Nobody accepts me. Nobody loves me. I have no more strength and no more ambition to seek friendship. I am left hopelessly alone.

I am completely forgotten like someone dead. I am merely a broken dish. (v. 12)

This feeling: I cannot contain myself, hold myself together. Everything seeps out of me. The bottom has dropped out of the vessel of my soul. Everything passes through me, and I am losing, losing, losing.

Helps in Overcoming Depression

The Bible clearly shows that God realizes that we have these feelings, and that he understands us when we do. This fact may be already of help in dealing with depression: we do not need to be ashamed of these feelings. They are not a flaw in our make-up or a discredit to the name *Christian*.

On the other hand, we should not sit on the pity pot and mope away all day long. At one time when my wife was rather depressed, she asked one of our teen-age sons, "What shall I do?" After a few minutes' reflection, he answered, "Above all, Mommy, do something! Don't just do nothing!" That was the right word for her at that moment.

In a way, each person is his or her own best doctor when it comes to curing depression. I know a lady who often suffers from depression without an apparent cause. This state prevents her from thinking clearly and acting objectively. Consequently, she has made for herself what she calls a "depression emergency kit." Like a doctor's prescription, she has written down instructions to herself, telling her what to do in case of a depression. First of all, she has a little box of cards with special Bible verses containing promises and assurance. She picks out a card and reads it aloud. Next, she makes herself a good cup of tea which she sips slowly while listening to her favorite music. She also has on hand an absorbing book which she has been eager to read, but which she has saved for this occasion. Afterward, she calls up a friend and combines the visit to her with a walk outdoors.

We must be experiencing a bit of self-love already when we combat depression by such a method.

I mentioned earlier Martin Luther's unhappy childhood and strict religious upbringing which caused him great difficulties in learning to love himself. He learned to regard self-love as a sinful and egotistic streak in man. From what we have learned about the relation between the lack of self-love and depression, it is no wonder that Martin Luther was sorely afflicted by depression. And through his own experiences, he is able to give us sound advice. I would like to share some of his suggestions with you, adding comments of my own:[14]

1. *Avoid being alone.* Luther states that isolation is poison for the depressed person, by which the devil attempts to keep the depressed under his spell. "Talk

LOVE YOURSELF / 61

among yourselves, so that I know I am surrounded by people," requested Luther in one of his table talks. He apparently asked this at a moment when he felt disheartened.

2. *Seek out people or entertainment which generate joy.* Joy is always pleasing to God, even though it may not always be of a religious nature. Enjoying a good play or movie is just as legitimate as taking a long walk in the woods.

3. *Sing and make music.* Here Luther emphasizes the active involvement necessary for a person to make music of his own rather than simply listening to it. He once advised an aristocrat who was despondent, "When you are sad and feeling discouraged, just tell yourself, 'Up! Up! I must play a song on the organ in praise of my Lord.' For the Scriptures assure us that God delights in song and playing musical instruments. So play upon the keys and give yourself to song until the gloomy thoughts are passed, just as David did. If the devil continues to pester you, reprimand him saying, 'be gone, Satan, I have to sing and play now for my Lord Jesus.'" Again, Luther refers not only to religious music here, but to music in general. Then God becomes the listener, and we give Him joy through our performance, a joy that lightens our own heavy hearts.

4. *Dismiss heavy thoughts.* Luther warns us of the danger of becoming engrossed by gloomy or despairing thoughts which tend to keep us awake at night, or which overwhelm us the first thing in the morning. He advises us either to express amusement at the devil or to scorn him, whichever works best for us, but by no means to give in to him on this matter: "But the very best thing would be to refuse to fight with the devil. Despise the depressive thoughts! Act as if you would not feel them! Think of something else and say: 'All right, devil, don't bother me. I have no time now to occupy myself with your thoughts. I must ride horseback, go places, eat, drink, and do this or that. Now I must be cheerful. Come again some other day.'"[15]

5. *Rely upon the promises of Scripture.* They encourage our mind to think positively, just as the lady did with her depression emergency kit. It might be especially helpful to learn by heart those verses which have helped us before. They are like rods and staffs comforting us when walking through the valley of the shadow of death, as Psalm 23 puts it.

6. *Seek consolation from others.* In a state of depression, we often make a mountain out of a molehill. A friend, however, sees things in the right perspective and recognizes the positive side which we cannot see

at the moment. It is impossible to lift ourselves up by pulling our own hair. We need the assistance of others to rescue us from the grip of despair. In turn we should ask ourselves if we are willing and able to help others just as God helped Elijah through a warm and assuring embrace, a good meal, and a quiet rest?

7. *Praise and thanksgiving.* These are powerful weapons against depression. We are reminded again of Nebuchadnezzar, who, when he raised his eyes to heaven and praised God, overcame the depression which had seized him. It helps to make a list of the things one is thankful for and then praise God by reading them aloud.

8. *Think of other depressed people.* This is rather a surprising suggestion by Luther, but it makes sense to me. It shakes us out of our self-centered sorrow in which we insist that no one else in the world suffers as much as we do.

9. *Exercise patience with yourself.* The word *exercise* is important here and also implies vigorous physical activity. Sometimes we must resign ourselves to the fact that life contains valleys and deserts that simply must be endured. Just as any other skill has to be acquired, we must also learn how to persevere during times of personal stress.[16]

I would like to add physical exercise in any form: jogging, swimming, dancing, or gardening. These all will help us practice patience with ourselves. Any sweat-producing activity—including sauna—that enables the entire skin surface to "weep," results in an amazingly quick recovery from depression.

10. *Believe in the blessing of depression.* Depression can be positive and fruitful even if it occurs over and over again. This advice of Luther contains such a profound insight that I would like to conclude by discussing it in more detail.

The Gift of Depression

The German word for depression is *Schwermut*. *Schwer* can mean heavy as well as difficult. *Mut* is the word for courage. Accordingly, the word *Schwermut* contains a positive message. It means the courage to be heavy-hearted, the courage to live with what is difficult.

Courage is involved in being depressed. There is such a thing as the gift of depression—a gift which enables us to live with what weighs heavily on us, with what is difficult. Once I heard an experienced psychiatrist say, "All people of worth and value have depressions." It requires a certain inner substance and depth of mind to be depressed. Young children, who have not yet attained such depth of mind, often do not become as depressed as adults may.

Suicide may result from an insufficient ability to be depressed.[17] It may be much easier for those ignoring the depths of their personality to cut the thread of life. The philosopher Landsberg made an assertion that deserves a few moments of quiet contemplation: "Often a man will kill himself because he cannot despair, because he cannot *want* to despair." Suicide, accordingly, results from being unable to experience true desperation, to become truly depressed. The suicidal person lacks the courage to feel weighed down. Luther's advice is indeed comforting and therapeutic: "Believe in the blessing of depression."

Creative people such as artists and musicians can be quite susceptible to depression, perhaps because the "courage to feel weighed down" is a prerequisite for creative productivity. It is no coincidence that the poet Rainer Maria Rilke, who passionately searched for the secret of creativity throughout his life, writes in a letter from Rome in May 1904:

We know only little, but this is a certainty which will not forsake us: we must hold on to what is difficult; it is good to be alone, for solitude is difficult; and since it is difficult, we have further grounds to do it.[18]

Note that Rilke associates the acceptance of what is difficult with the acceptance of solitude.

In another letter of August 12th 1904, Rilke points out that depression—just like self-love—in working upon us, transforms us and produces change. When we read his lines, we are again reminded of Luther's advice to have patience with ourselves:

So you must not be frightened if a sadness rises up before you larger than any you have ever seen; if a restiveness, like light and cloud-shadows, passes over your hands and over all you do. You must think that something is happening with you, that life has not forgotten you, that it holds you in its hand; it will not let you fall. Why do you want to shut out of your life any agitation, any pain, any melancholy, since you really do not know what these states are working upon you? Why do you want to persecute yourself with the question whence all this may be coming and whither it is bound since you know that you are in the midst of transitions and wished for nothing so much as to change? If there is anything morbid in your processes, just remember that sickness is the means by which an organism frees itself of foreign matter; so one must just help it to be sick, to have its whole sickness and break out with it, for that is its progress. In you, dear sir, so much is now happen-

ing; you must be patient as a sick man and confident as a convalescent; for perhaps you are both.[19]

The poet Owlglass reports the following conversation between two friends, one of whom was suffering from a deep depression. The first one asks, "Why are you so depressed, my friend?" The other one replies, "I wish I could fly away and leave all my burdens behind me. I am so full of them and so heavy-hearted because of them. Why can't I be lighthearted?" His wise friend responds with the counter-question, "Why are you not empty-hearted?"

Given the choice, which would we rather be: lighthearted and empty, or heavy-hearted and full? I believe it is possible to love ourselves with a full heart, even if it is heavy, while we could hardly love ourselves with an empty heart.

Some readers certainly must have been puzzled when I dealt with the depression of King Saul. Here the Bible uses a very strange expression. It describes depression as an "evil spirit from God" (1 Sam. 16:23). An evil spirit from God?

This is authentic biblical thinking: depression can be a part of God's plan. In the story of Saul, depression was an instrument which God used to bring David into the king's palace. To believe in the blessing of depression means to recognize that God uses even depression to fulfill his plans.

There is a God-related depression, a 'godly grief,' as the Apostle Paul calls it. "When God makes you feel sorry enough to turn to him an be saved, you don't have anything to feel bad about" (II Cor. 7:10). Or, as the Living Bible translates this passage, "For God sometimes uses sorrow in our lives to help us turn away from sin and seek eternal life."

However, this 'turn' resulting from depression does not happen by itself. It needs the work of faith which consciously relates depression to God and which receives it out of His hands. Otherwise this turn may not take place: "But when this world makes you feel sorry, it can cause your death" (2 Cor. 7:10).

This is what happened to Saul. He did not succeed in relating the evil spirit to God and then change his life. Instead, he became increasingly entangled in his depressive moods. Finally, not even David's music alleviated the depression. Instead, Saul began to harbor threats against David: "The next day the Lord let an evil spirit take control of Saul, and he began acting like a crazy man inside his house. David came to play the harp for Saul as usual, but this time Saul had a spear in his hand. Saul thought, 'I'll pin David to the wall'" (1 Sam. 18:10-11). Depression can lead to sin when we do not relate it to God. It can become "worldly grief" that leads to death.

The counterpart to Saul is the depression Jesus had in the garden of Gethsemane when telling his disciples, "I am so sad that I feel as if I am dying" (Matthew 26:38). In his prayer, however, he succeeded relating his depression to God. He opened himself to receiving resources that came from outside: "'Father, if you will, please don't make me suffer by having me drink from this cup. But do what you want, and not what I want.' Then an angel from heaven came to help him" (Luke 22:42-43).

There is a depression in which we encounter God, in which we are held by God. This experience gives us the courage to love ourselves as we are, *with* our depressions, and be cheerful even with a heavy heart. It reflects a depth of faith which the Apostle Paul expressed with the paradoxical statement: "But in everything and in every way we show that we truly are God's servants. ... and we are always happy, even in times of suffering" (2 Cor. 6:4,10).

I wish so much that the girl whom I mentioned in the beginning and who could not believe and accept that she was beautiful would read this book. Maybe it would help her to work on herself and undergo the painful-joyful learning process of self-love.

On that day when my wife and I talked with her, we had too little time to do more than show her a first step. However, we did not let her go without laying our hands on her and blessing her in Christ's name.

In our ministry, we have experienced the effectiveness of this action in the counseling process again and again. Only Christ-centered counseling is truly client-centered.

We do not know where this beautiful girl is today. But we remember the words which were given to us for her. They were the very same quoted above by the Apostle Paul. We blessed her that she might establish herself as a servant of God—that even in times of suffering, she would always be happy.

LOVE IS A FEELING TO BE LEARNED

In India, one tells this legend about the creation of man and woman:

When he had finished creating the man, the Creator realized that he had used up all the physical elements. There was nothing substantial, dense, or durable left over to create the woman.

After thinking for a long time, the Creator took:

the roundness of the moon, the agility of a clinging vine, and the trembling of grass,

the slenderness of a reed and the beauty of blossoming flowers,

the lightness of leaves and the cheerfulness of rays of sunshine,

the tears of clouds and the instability of the winds,

the fearfulness of a rabbit and the vanity of a peacock,

the softness of a bird's breast and the hardness of a diamond,

the sweetness of honey and the cruelty of a tiger,

the heat of burning fire and the chilliness of snow,

the chatter of a magpie and the song of a nightingale,

the deceitfulness of a crane and the faithfulness of a mother lion.

Mixing all these yielding elements together, the Creator created the woman and gave her to the man.

After one week the man came back and said:

"Lord, the creature that you have given to me makes my life unhappy. She talks without ceasing and torments me intolerably so that I have no rest. She insists that I pay attention to her all the time, and so my hours are wasted. She cries about every little thing and leads an idle life. I have come to give her back to you because I can't live with her."

The Creator said: "All right." And he took her back.

After a week had passed, the man came back to the Creator and said: "Lord, my life is so empty since I gave that creature back to you. I always think of her—how she danced and sang, how she looked at me out of the corner of her eye, how she talked and then snuggled close to me. She was so beautiful to look at and so soft to touch. I so much liked to hear her laugh. Please give her back to me."

The Creator said: "All right." And he gave her back.

But three days later the man came back again and said:

"Lord, I don't know—I just can't explain it, but after all my experience with this creature, I've come to the conclusion that she causes me more trouble than pleasure. I pray thee, take her back again! I can't live with her!"

But the Creator said: "Go away, quickly, for I have had enough! Live to the best of your ability!"

The man answered: "But I can't live with her!"

"And you can't live without her either!" replied the Creator.

And he turned his back to the man and continued his work.

The man said in desperation: "What shall I do? I can't live *with* her and I can't live *without* her!"

***

Love is a feeling to be learned.

It is anxiety and contentment.

It is deep yearning and hostility.

It is pleasure and pain.

There is not one without the other.

Happiness is only a part of love—this is what has to be learned.

Suffering also belongs to love. This is the mystery of love, its beauty and its burden.

Love is a feeling to be learned.

***

It caused Sylvia almost physical pain to give up her dream. But now she was sure: this was the end of it.

Before she had met 'him', she had had a dream image of her future husband. He would be tall, slim, a good athlete, intelligent, witty, a university graduate, and a few years older than she. Of course, he would also be a lover of music and poetry, possibly a professor of English literature or religion, or he would hold a well-paid job with the government.

When she passed a florist shop and saw the dark-red roses in the window, Sylvia imagined how it would be someday when someone would bring her such gorgeous roses as a declaration of his love.

Gone was the dream! 'He' was so different. There was absolutely nothing exciting about him. When he had asked her out on their first date, she had prayed in her heart: "Please, Lord, not him! He's not the one I want to marry!"

She had never been interested in technical things, and that was all he talked about because he was a construction engineer. He also was rather dull. He didn't even think about bringing her roses. He didn't bring her anything. He just showed up and there he was.

He was so down to earth and so sober.

Not that he was without feeling, just that the expression of his emotions irritated her. She couldn't rely upon them because they could change so quickly. One minute he was spontaneous and enthusiastic, and the next he was wooden and inexpressive. When she longed for a tender word he offered her a kiss instead, while at the same time he talked about sports or his studies.

Everything was reason and determination with him. He called her foolish and sentimental when she put more faith in her intuition than in his rational judgment.

Why can't a man be like a woman?

Sometimes she wanted to be like a porcupine, roll together and display her quills to make him understand in a thorny way that moonlight did not increase her desire for closeness.

In his presence she felt the desire to retreat into a fortress of freedom and hoist the flag of independence.

Yet, Sylvia did not reject him. Not yet, she thought, maybe later on.

Later on, after about half a year or so, a few things dawned on her. She began to understand that a young man who offers his girlfriend a book about his own interests might be more serious than someone who brings her roses.

The book shows her: "I want to share something with you which moves my heart. I want to offer you an important part in my life. I want to know what you think. It is important to me to know what you think."

To her astonishment she discovered one day that she had stopped to look at a bridge. For the first time she saw the beauty of its suspension and of its distinct contours. Another time she stood and watched as the steel beams for a skyscraper were hoisted upwards, and she thought "I should show this to him."

Being understood was no longer the only thing that mattered. She herself had begun to understand. She had learned the first lesson of love: to let go of one's imaginings and not let them get in the way of happiness.

Love is a special feeling—a feeling to be learned.

***

If this special feeling of love is not learned, if romance in the relationship between the sexes is not permitted, sex and love become synonymous and interchangeable. To some extent, this is still true in

Africa. Sex is called love and love is called sex. "I loved a girl," means, "I went to bed with a girl." For those who have not learned the special feeling of love, there is only everything or nothing. The *in-between* does not exist.

The consequences of this attitude are terrifying. The woman becomes little more than an instrument for reproduction, a well-equipped incubator. She is not a person, but a thing which can be traded, bought and sold, given and taken back, exchanged and disposed of, she is an inferior being without a will of her own, and she is always subjected to male desires. In cultures of little sexual restraint the woman ultimately turns into a thing, a matter, an object.

All of us have to learn how to love, how to appreciate the beauty of the *in-between* and the joy of the *preliminary*.

Sylvia said: "Our relationship was relaxed, without tension; there was the ease of something not yet final, and that is what I appreciated the most. This ease also provided the promise for greatness and depth. This calmness, more than anything else, strengthened our friendship.

"Although the *in-between* was relaxed, we did experience the pain of longing and the agony of the un-

known. Pain and agony, however, were simultane-
ously joined by deeply felt happiness."

***

Did you hear that? Pain and suffering! Popular songs
and movies lie to us when they suggest that happiness can be attained without suffering. Here lies the
cause for the failure of many relationships, for the
disappointment and agony, yes, even for the shal-
lowness and shipwreck of many marriages: to think
that love can grow and live without suffering.

Love and suffering do not exclude each other.
Rather, they bring each other about.

Sexual problems may arise from refusing to accept
suffering, from wanting to skip the *in-between* stage
with its tension and uncertainty. And thus *love* becomes an empty and meaningless word.

To accept suffering and hardship willingly, on the
other hand, provides love with meaning and life with
depth.

In a letter to a young woman, the German poet
Rainer Maria Rilke wrote:

*To young people I would always like to stress this—we have
to hold on to that which weighs on us ... We must go into life
at such depth that life lays on top of us and becomes a burden:
lust is not supposed to surround us, but life ... If for many*

people life has suddenly become easier, more careless and joyful, it is only because they have ceased to take it seriously, to bear it in reality, and to feel and fulfill it with their own being ... We are asked to learn to love and deal with that which weighs on us. Therein lie the friendly forces, the hands that shape us.[20]

It pays to suffer love's grief.

We must not attempt to simply wipe out suffering, especially not if it takes a toll on us. If we accept and live with it, suffering can become a source of wealth, of depth, of growth, of fulfillment, and yes, even of happiness.

In contradiction to the popular songs and movies of our time, I stress once more: it pays to suffer love's grief.

***

Michael sat and thought.

It finally happened. His girlfriend had broken up with him.

He really couldn't understand why. True, he had made mistakes. Maybe he had even taken too much for granted—too much and too soon.

He had felt all along that she had never taken their relationship as seriously as he had. Maybe she was afraid to do so.

Though they were both the same age, he had always felt inferior and unsure of himself in her presence. Sometimes he had the impression that she was years older while he felt like a baby with a beard.

Why can't a man be like a woman?

He had to accept her decision. It was painful and his heart ached, but he didn't want to drown out the pain or simply cover it up. He wanted to take the pain seriously.

So he sat and thought.

Maybe this was the purpose of suffering. Perhaps this was supposed to teach him the distinction between the real and the artificial, and above all the art of sacrifice.

A most essential ingredient for love is the ability to give up and to let go. Mastering this art makes love's grief worthwhile.

Not just for love's sake. I believe that the survival of humankind will depend on our ability to learn the art of sacrifice, on our willingness to give up not only our unattainable dreams, but also those wishes and desires we could realize and fulfill.

Suffering makes immature love grow into mature love. Immature love is egotistic, for it does not want to learn. That is the kind of love children have, demanding and wanting—and wanting instantaneously.

It cannot bear tension and tolerate obstacles. It is needy and greedy, and it tries to dictate.

As Michael sat and thought, he realized that the greatest proof of his love to his girlfriend was to give her the liberty to say "no." Mature love does not dominate others, but it lets go. It sets free.

Suffering transformed Michael's love into a new dimension.

It pays to suffer love's grief, for nothing prepares us better for marriage. Marital love has learned to surrender and to sacrifice.

In marriage we give up the notions of *yours* or *mine* in favor of *ours*.

The word *our* is always associated with making sacrifices:

letting go of one's partner as he or she goes to work,

giving up free time and independent planning for the family's sake,

giving up things one could have afforded working as a single person,

making sacrifices for the sake of the children,

and perhaps the hardest sacrifice of all: letting go of the children themselves as they start to go their own ways.

***

Maybe therein lies the root of the generation gap problem. Parents who have not learned the art of sacrifice as part of their love are unable to let go of their own children. They behave like chickens who hatch duck eggs and then stand at the edge of the pond cackling and squawking as the young ducklings swim away.

Such parents have yet to learn a lot, and their children need to be patient with them. Mark Twain once said: "When I was sixteen, I thought my dad was hopeless. When I was twenty, I was surprised to discover that he had made progress."

However, the exact opposite may apply as well. Sometimes parents say "no" to teach love that sacrifices. And by obeying their parents, children may learn the art of letting go. That ability will be invaluable when they face the reality of love while shaping their own marriages and educating their own children.

***

The art of letting go and of abandoning selfish desires is also the secret of happiness in a single person's life. The giving up of oneself is as important for singles as it is for the married.

Those who learn this art will never feel alone even if they remain single. Those who do not learn it will always feel alone even though they are married.

Whether married or single, we face the same task: *to live a fulfilled life in spite of many unfulfilled desires.*[21]

Love is a feeling singles need to learn as well. They do not need to give up love, but they need to learn love which gives up—just as married individuals must learn it. The desire to be married, moreover, might be an important prerequisite for a happy single life.

Though we face the same task, whether married or single, let us not mistakenly think that our present state will last forever. Let us not burden our hearts with the fear of finality and inevitability.

Marriage can be a task for a limited time, for it can end suddenly with the death of one partner. Being single may also be but a passing task.

God does not like decisions for a lifetime which we make out of resignation and disappointment. He wants us to live our life now, one day at a time, and to discover all its joyous possibilities with confidence and courage.

***

Evelyn sat on the train with her eyes shut so that the other passengers would think she was asleep. But her heart sang with the rhythm of the wheels on the rails: "He loves me. I shall be his wife. He shall be my husband."

No, she would never be able to understand it. She couldn't even explain it—not to her mother or even to her girlfriend. She knew in her heart from the moment they looked at each other with the expression in their eyes: "I do mean you, you alone, you for my entire life."

How did Carl succeed? Had he outwitted her by pretending at first not to be interested in her? Had his methods been cleverer than those of others?

No, he hadn't even considered methods. His attitude had not been "cautiously take the little finger first and the hand will surely follow."

A rather insignificant gesture allowed her to appreciate his way of being a friend. During her first year at college, he had asked her out on their first date. It was planned for a Saturday evening, and he knew that on weekends she usually went home to see her family and friends. When she accepted his invitation to attend a play with him, he expressly thanked her for giving up her trip home.

Through this gesture she understood for the first time—he does not just want to spend an enjoyable evening, he is not just looking for a pleasant companion for a few hours. With his invitation he really means *me*.

Love is a feeling to be learned, and Evelyn knew in her heart it could never be learned by having sex. She would never have reached the certainty she now had. Just as loud drums drown out the main tune played by flutes, sex would have deafened her ears to the low and gentle overtones so essential for making the right choice.

Carl would not have heard the song of the nightingale, nor seen the trembling of grass, the agility of a clinging vine, or the cheerfulness of rays of sunshine; nor would he have felt the instability of the winds, or the softness of a bird's breast.

They would have missed the beauty of the *in-between*, the pain of waiting, the joy of suspense, and the suffering which made them so happy.

Evelyn knew: sex would have deprived their love from the potential for growth. They would have picked the blossoms in April and therefore been unable to harvest the seasoned apples later.

Love does not grow out of sex. Love must grow into sex. Love must be there first.

For Evelyn love meant above all trust and faithfulness, fellowship and common experiences, shared hopes and concerns. It called for a reliable and lasting relationship. For her, love and permanence were inseparable.

Could it be, Evelyn thought, while the train was bringing her closer and closer to her friend—could it be that consenting to premarital sex represses inner feelings and longings? Could it be that it does not lead to passion, but rather to coldness and unresponsiveness, or even to a calculating indifference?

***

Carl felt that sexual abstinence, more than anything, had helped his love for Evelyn to mature. Like a dam which helps to turn the power of water into electricity, restraint helps to turn the power of sex into love.

Two characteristics about Evelyn had helped Carl especially: her appeal and her modesty. One without the other does not suffice. He had never before understood their wonderful complementarity.

Her appeal had taught him to pay a price and to make a sacrifice for his love.

Her modesty had guided his interest beyond her body toward her soul. This in turn had helped him—

accustomed as he was to living within the realm of will and reason—to discover his own soul.

Maybe women do need to mentor men in this realm, Carl thought.

Had she been appealing and not modest, she would have led him toward adventure, but not toward marriage.

Appeal without modesty would have tempted him to fulfill his desires at the lowest possible price.

Had she given in to his desires, to him she would have lost her appeal. Indeed, he had secretly hoped for her resistance because he loved her and did not want to lose her.

Refusing sex was a greater proof of her love for him than consenting to sex. Had she permitted sexual relations, she would have harmed their love.

***

Sex can harm love. Sex can kill love. Therefore, love needs to be protected.

A Bible verse, Genesis 2:25, deserves our attention in this matter: "Although the man and his wife were both naked, they were not ashamed."

Naked and not ashamed.

Naked implies much more than just wearing no clothes. *Naked* means to stand—bare and undis-

guised—in front my partner without pretending anything and without hiding anything. Naked means:
seeing my partner in an all-encompassing reality, *exposing* myself to my partner in an all-encompassing reality, and still, *feeling* not ashamed.

Naked and not ashamed.

This ultimate goal of mature love, however, is
promised only to those who—as stated in the previ-
ous verse—have left father and mother and cling to
each other. In other words, it is promised only to
those who have been publicly and legally married.

These two—not the two before or outside of marriage—become one flesh.

These two—not the two before or outside of marriage—shall succeed in this tremendously difficult
task: to face each other as they really are and to live
with each other—naked and yet not ashamed.

Naked and not ashamed—this is the Biblical meaning of *to know*, as *Adam knew Eve, his wife.*

Such *knowing* is impossible outside of marriage. If it
is tried beforehand, love is harmed or even destroyed.

Therefore, love needs to be not only learned, love
needs to be also protected.

***

Love needs to be protected by God's will. We cannot protect love by listening to human reason.

Unfortunately, it has become a fashion to question God's will in the name of love.

"Did God say that?" they ask, as the serpent asked Eve in the Garden of Eden.

"Is it not love," they ask, "to shorten the torment of waiting by encouraging premarital sex?"

"Is it not love," they ask, "allowing your spouse to have sexual relations with someone else, provided they love each other?"

I remember a film shown in Germany during the time of Hitler. It told the story of a doctor whose wife had an incurable disease. The film showed in all detail how she was tormented by her illness. Finally, her husband killed her with an overdose of sedatives. When he was put on trial for her murder, he defended himself by saying: "I loved my wife."

God's commandment "Thou shalt not kill" was questioned in the name of love.

The film, shown in 1940, served Hitler as a psychological preparation for putting to death the incurable and insane, and for killing those whom he judged unworthy of living. The result was the murder of six million Jews in the gas chambers of the concentration and extermination camps of the Third Reich.

If we seek to define the standards of love ourselves, we fall into the hands of the devil. When Germany questioned the commandment "Thou shalt not kill" (Exodus 20:13 KJV) in the name of love, she fell into the hands of the devil. When we question the commandment "Thou shalt not commit adultery" (Exodus 20:14 KJV) in the name of love, we equally fall into the hands of the devil.

Since we cannot fully comprehend love by ourselves, it has to be protected by the one who is *love* himself. There can never be a contradiction between love and God's will. True love can never violate a commandment of God.

We always harm others when we break a commandment, even if we cannot see it right away in our present situation. But God is greater than our situation. He looks far beyond what I can see. He has the film of my whole life in view, not just the snapshot of my present situation.

The life view offers a different image than the snapshot. Let me illustrate this by the case of François and Cecile, the young African couple whose correspondence with me is published in the book, *I Loved a Girl.*

Those who have read *I Loved A Girl* will know that François and Cecile eloped because they saw no other way out of their situation. And thus, they physically consummated their marriage before they were legally married.

Who can blame them? Humanly, we can understand their actions in such a difficult situation.

And yet, today they regret their actions of the past. They now agree that the consummation of their marriage before the wedding has been more harmful to their love than helpful.

Taking a snapshot out of context may turn a premarital or extramarital surrender into a beautiful lie, or make a gentle murder appear as an expression of love to our understanding. If the image of the entire film of life is in full view, however, the matter may look very different.

When examining a devastated life, one inevitably finds that the chaos had started with the transgression of one of God's commandments.

Jesus says: "If you obey me, I will keep loving you" (John 15:10).

We cannot love our neighbor unless we love Jesus. We cannot love Jesus unless we obey His commandments.

Only the one who truly loves is capable of obeying.

Only the one who obeys can truly love.

"We show our love for God by obeying his commandments, and they are not hard to follow" (I John 5:3).

They do not burden us, but support us. They do not weigh us down, but strengthen us. They do not invalidate us, but let us mature. Keeping the commandments is actually much simpler than transgressing them. Life becomes much more difficult and complicated if we try to determine for ourselves what is good and what is bad.

***

Many people claim that premarital sex has become customary among teenagers today, and some compelling statistics illustrate this trend.

So what?

Since when are Christians guided by statistics? Since when do the actions of a majority show our way? "But you are God's chosen and special people" (I Peter 2:9). Christians are not shy animals who have to rely on camouflage for their survival. On the contrary, we will not survive unless we show our colors.

Dietrich Bonhoeffer once said: "Only the extraordinary is essentially Christian."

***

Let me conclude by telling you about my conversation with Karin, as we shall call her.

During our talk Karin assured me several times that she had been physically involved with her boyfriend, but that they had never gone *all the way*.

I did not ask any questions. Nevertheless, the next day Karin came back and wanted to know what the expression *going all the way* really meant. I said, "Generally, it means: full sexual intercourse; the insertion of the penis into the vagina." Karin hesitated for a moment. Then she said softly: "If this is true, then we did go all the way."

Then she could not hold back her emotions any longer: "Please do not think that I lied to you yesterday. You are the first who told me what that expression specifically means. 'Be careful and don't make anything dirty!' That was all my mother said when I had my first menstruation."

"That was the extent of my sex education. Why do they all beat around the bush? 'Don't go all the way! Don't go too far!' But what *too far* really means, no one ever told me. I wondered whether embracing or kissing went *too far?*"

Then Karin challenged me. She wanted an accurate definition of *going too far*. I thought of the many talks

I had with young people who assured me, sometimes in tears, that neither one had intended to go all the way, but that they could not stop after a certain point.

I responded (and I ask those who know of a better response to correct me), "lying down together and undressing even slightly may already be going too far, may reach the point where stopping becomes impossible."

"Who should be in charge of slowing down, the woman or the man?" asked Karin.

"A general rule cannot be established. I would, however, offer this as a guideline: the partner who is perceptively more conscious should help the other one. Slapping fingers may show love more meaningfully than French-kissing. Respect for one another grows and love deepens. Going all the way, on the other hand, turns out to short-circuit the relationship. *Going all the way* will not go all the way, nor will it go half the way. It will not even offer a beginning, instead a beginning in the opposite direction. Only love goes *all the way*. But the very feeling of love that wants to be expressed, that wants to find fulfillment, is harmed or even destroyed."

"Can sex harm love?"

"Oh yes, Karin. It certainly can."

A student couple expecting a child out of wedlock wrote to me: "Isn't all that matters that we did it in love?"

I answered: "Love? Perhaps, but only a limited and self-centered kind of love. Is it love for the baby for whom no proper home is prepared? Is it love for your partner whose professional career is now in jeopardy? What could have been prepared with patience and wisdom must now be rushed. Maybe you solved one problem—you released the sexual tension. But you created a multitude of others— wedding, home, financial support, professional ambitions …"

"You see, Karin," I added, "Sex can harm love. Therefore, God protects love by confining sex exclusively to marriage."

Karin thought for a while. Then she asked: "Isn't it love which encourages most girls to engage in a physical relationship?"

"Perhaps what they think of as love. But rarely will such first physical encounters lead to marriage. Many a broken life started this way. And let me therefore reiterate emphatically: even a first and only episode of sexual intercourse can result in a pregnancy."

"But," Karin said, "isn't it her own negligence if the girl becomes pregnant? When I worried about that, my boyfriend reassuringly told me that he would watch out. At first, I did not know what he meant by watching out. Now I know. He made sure he withdrew before he ejaculated. But you see, that way I did not get any satisfaction, and I thought we had not gone *all the way*."

I was glad that Karin spoke so openly. Such a method of birth control provides some pleasure for men, but hardly for women. Interrupted intercourse—interrupted for the girl—may cause frigidity later in her life. She may even develop an aversion, a feeling of disgust or loathsomeness toward anything sexual, and thus toward marriage.

And so, love is harmed again. The method of withdrawal is not only unaesthetic but also unsafe, for the moment of withdrawal can easily be misjudged.

"Is there any absolutely safe means of birth control?" Karin asked.

I don't know of any. Condoms can break. IUDs can be incorrectly fitted. The so-called calendar method, determining the phase of infertility by merely counting the days in a woman's menstrual cycle, is not safe either, for her periods may not be regular."

"And how about the pill?"

"The pill presents additional challenges. It has to be prescribed, and it is only effective when taken daily between two menstrual cycles. Missing only one day renders the pill useless. Carrying it in your purse when going out to a dance so as to having it available when needed, makes the pill completely ineffective.

"Furthermore, swallowing a pill daily over a long period of time can influence a young woman's organism negatively, particularly her delicate hormonal balance. As soon as she stops taking the pill, her ability to conceive may increase drastically. Incidents of releasing more than one egg cell have been observed. This may result in pregnancies of multiple embryos. Or, on the other hand, the normal release of egg cells may be delayed following cessation of the pill so that the woman may become sterile indefinitely. These adverse reactions are not common, but they are completely unpredictable and can bear tragic consequences.

"I once heard a young woman say: 'If I would take the pill regularly, calculatingly, in anticipation of a possible sex adventure, I would feel like a prostitute.'"

"Wouldn't *making out* solve all problems?"

"What do you mean with *making out*?"

She explained: "not just holding hands and kissing, but mutually manipulating the sexual organs until both partners reach orgasm. In this way sexual pleasure can be experienced without fear of pregnancy and also without having to use contraceptives or counting days.

I know of Christians who calm their conscience by doing this and then claiming they have not engaged in full intercourse."

I confirmed this observation. I know many Christians who believe that they can outmaneuver the commandments of God. After all, they have not gone *all the way*!

This appears to be an ideal solution, but it really is a dead-end road. I had to explain to Karin that mutual stimulation used as a method of birth control is not absolutely safe, either. Exposing the vagina even to the smallest amount of semen may still fertilize an egg cell. And besides, exploring each other physically often will not stop until full sexual union takes place.

Another fact is still more significant. For women, sexual pleasure may be experienced on two levels: one is somewhat superficial and not fully satisfying, and the other is gratifying and deeply fulfilling. The latter, however, is generally only possible in marriage, for it requires a harmonious relationship with the same partner over a long period of time. Women who have reached the second level of deeply gratifying sexual pleasure regard the first one as childish and immature.

Once more, sex without marriage takes place at the expense of love. Those who want sex without marriage can neither learn nor protect love. They deprive themselves of the invaluable experience of growing and of becoming mature.

I would also like to point out briefly that *making out*, as Karin calls it, may lead to a habit of masturbation when the partner is gone. This form of self-gratification is not necessarily an illness, but it may be a symptom of loneliness and of losing sexual self-control. Gaining control of your sexual desires will increase your ability to love with your heart and devote yourself to the need and the happiness of others. If you suffer from lacking friends and acquaintances, if you have difficulty opening up to others, masturbation may be a cry for help. Then you should not remain alone, but seek the guidance of an experienced counselor who can help you from revolving around yourself and open up to others.[22]

Karin asked again: "Why didn't someone tell me these things before?"

I responded: "Karin, I also often wonder about the reason for this strange silence. Perhaps it comes from a bad conscience, or perhaps from a feeling of inadequacy, especially after experiencing failure. Karin, will you become a better mother to your own children than your mother has been to you?"

"It's true," she said. "I had a bad conscience when I gave in to the desires of my boyfriend. You mustn't believe that I just let it all happen. I fought it although I also wanted it. Deep down in my soul, it all hurt me. I pretended to be happy, but I really felt like weeping."

"Karin," I said, "if only you had wept, he probably would not have asked you to give in. You would have challenged him as a man, and he would have wanted to protect you. Since you pretended to be happy, he tried to make you happy. And yet, he harmed you."

"I can't understand it," she said, "I did not want it, but he did. And when I gave in he lost interest. For him it was the end. For me it was a beginning. He just can't understand that."

After a pause Karin continued: "When I listen to you, it becomes obvious that sex without marriage is foolish. But whenever I find myself overcome with

desire, a host of clever good reasons just the opposite come to mind."

"That is quite common and happens to many people," I responded. "Arguments, no matter how
clever, won't help in the end. We need a grip that is
larger than our understanding. This grip is the will of
our creator, of the one who also created our sexual
desire and our longing for union."

"And how do I get to know God's will?"

"The will of God," I said, "is contained in the following simple sentence: 'Therefore shall a man will
leave his father and his mother, and shall cleave unto
his wife: and they shall be one flesh' (KJV). This sentence is written in Genesis 2:24 and repeated three
times in the New Testament. The word *leave* refers to
a public and legal act which today is carried out by
the wedding ceremony. The expression *be one flesh* is
mentioned in the Bible exclusively in the context of
marriage. This means: According to God's will, the
sexual union belongs within marriage as an expression of conjugal love. Only the one who *leaves* is also
able to *cleave* and experience the ultimate fulfillment
in the sense of *be one flesh*."

Karin objected: "Isn't that simply too taxing in our
time so driven and dominated by sex?"

"Karin, do you really believe the past was that different? Nonetheless, the challenge remains in our time: Keeping God's commandments requires much less effort than transgressing them. They are no burden, but a comfort. Life becomes much more complicated for those who claim knowledge about good and evil. Only the obedient are truthful and therein also joyous."

"Well," Karin said sadly, "I can no longer attain this joyous feeling. This insight comes too late for me."

I had to contradict her. As a conclusion to our conversation, I told Karin what I would like to say to all who feel like her:

Love is a feeling to be learned. What is most difficult, perhaps, is the ability to let oneself be loved, unconditionally and without qualifications; to let oneself be loved by the God who knows of no *too late*. He is the Almighty. Through his forgiveness, he can even make things that have happened be *undone*. No one needs to continue life with a wounded soul. The opportunity of a new beginning exists for everyone.

If you would like to take this step toward a new beginning, let me give you twofold advice:

First, since it is hard to succeed on your own, get an experienced spiritual counselor as a guide.

Secondly, do not stop halfway, but make this a completely new beginning. Here you can really to *go all the way*. Clean up not only in matters of sex, but also in other dark areas. Do not confess the transgressions of only one commandment, but bring all of them to light.

Your failures and downfalls in the realm of sex may very well be based on disregarding the will of God in other areas of your life.

Jesus says: "He who comes to me I will not cast out" (John 6:37).

For love is a feeling we *may* learn.

Quiet Waters Publications
P.O. Box 34, Bolivar MO 65613-0034
http://www.quietwaterspub.com
Email: QWP@usa.net

I Loved A Girl

By Walter Trobisch
'Last Friday, I loved a girl—or as you would put it, I committed adultery.' This deeply moving story of a young African couple is Walter Trobisch's first book. It has become a classic with its frank answers to frank questions about sex and love. Its tremendous worldwide success led Walter and Ingrid Trobisch to leave their missionary post in Cameroun and start an international ministry as marriage and family counselors.
ISBN 1-931475-01-6

I Married You

By Walter Trobisch
Set in a large African city, this story covers only four days in the life of Walter and Ingrid Trobisch. Nothing in this book is fiction. All the stories have really happened. The people involved are still living today. The direct, sensitive, and compassionate narrative presents Christian marriage as a dynamic triangle.
ISBN 0-9663966-6-9

On Our Way Rejoicing

By Ingrid Trobisch
Ingrid Trobisch, tells the story of what happens when God takes away the father of ten children. A whole family is called to service and sent into the world. The story surges with movement, partings and reunion, sorrows and joys, adventure

and romance, shining courage, and above all, the warm love that knits together a large Christian family.

ISBN 0-9663966-2-6

The Adventures Of Pumpelhoober

By David Trobisch, illustrated by Eva Bruchmann
"In Austria they call someone who has a lot of bad luck, 'Pumpelhoober.' I, too, often have bad luck," Walter and Ingrid Trobisch's nine year old son David explains his nickname. This humorous children's book tells the story of the Trobisch family in Africa from the perspective of a child.

ISBN 0-9663966-4-2

A Book of Life: Spiritual Journaling in the Twenty-First Century

By Katrine Trobisch Stewart
Katrine Stewart's insights into the art of journal keeping entertain as well as challenge us to sit down and begin our very own "book of life" in word and image. The author describes fun and practical ways in which to capture our fragmented modern lives and also emphasizes the role of the journal as a time-tested tool for spiritual discernment.

ISBN 0-9663966-8-5

Footnotes

¹ "Loving Myself" reprinted by permission of Harper and Row. ©1976 by Ulrich Schaffer.

² Dr. Guido Gröger, unpublished letter to Walter Trobisch, 1967.

³ Romano Guardini, *Die Annahme seiner selbst. Den Menschen erkennt nur, wer von Gott weiß* (Mainz: Matthias-Grünewald Verlag, 1993) 5ᵗʰ ed.

⁴ Unless otherwise indicated, all Biblical citations are quoted from *The Holy Bible. Contemporary English Version* (New York: American Bible Society, 1995).

⁵ See the exegesis of Leviticus 19:18 by Martin Noth in *Das Alte Testament Deutsch* (Göttingen: Vandenhoeck and Ruprecht, 1962) p. 122.

⁶ Hermann Hesse, *Steppenwolf* (New York: Holt, Rinehart and Winston, 1961) p. 10.

⁷ Cf. Rudolf Affemann, *Geschlechtserziehung in der modernen Welt*, Gütersloh, p. 117: "Nur wer genügend er selbst ist, kann von sich absehen." "Only he who is sufficiently himself can divert attention from himself."

⁸ Theodor Bovet, *Die Liebe ist in unserer Mitte* (Tübingen: Katzmann Verlag) p. 177.

⁹ Walter Trobisch, *I Loved a Girl* (Bolivar: Quiet Waters Publications, 2001).

¹⁰ Paul Tournier, *A Place for You* (New York: Harper and Row, 1968) *p.66*.

¹¹ Ibid.

¹² Ingrid Trobisch, *The Joy of Being a Woman and What a Man Can Do* (Bolivar: Quiet Waters Publications, 2000).

¹³ Walter Uhsadel, "Der depressive Mensch in theologischer Sicht," *Wege zum Menschen* (August 1966), p. 310.

¹⁴ As quoted by August Hardeland, *Geschichte der Speciellen Seelsorge* (Germany, 1893).

¹⁵ *Ibid.* Martin Luther in a letter of November 22, 1532, to Johannes von Stockhausen.

[16] Walter Trobisch, *Martin Luther's Quiet Time* and *Spiritual Dryness* (Bolivar: Quiet Waters Publications, 1998).

[17] See *Wege zum Menschen*, op. cit., p. 266.

[18] Rainer Maria Rilke, *Briefe an einen jungen Dichter* (Stuttgart: Insel Nr. 406) p. 35.

[19] Rainer Maria Rilke, *Letters to a Young* Poet (New York: W.W. Norton, 1954), p. 53.

[20] Rainer Maria Rilke, *Briefe* (Frankfurt am Main: Insel, 1978) p. 103f.

[21] Dietrich Bonhoeffer, *Brevier* (Chr. Kaiser Verlag) p. 339.

[22] Cf. Ingrid and Walter Trobisch *My Beautiful Feeling.* (Bolivar: Quiet Waters Publications, 1998).

Breinigsville, PA USA
18 August 2010
243815BV00002B/8/A